DOING WHAT
IS RIGHT

PEACE·AND·JUSTICE·SERIES 7

DOING WHAT IS RIGHT

What the Bible Says About Covenant and Justice

LOIS BARRETT

HERALD PRESS
Scottdale, Pennsylvania
Kitchener, Ontario

Library of Congress Cataloging-in-Publication Data

Barrett, Lois.
    Doing what is right : what the Bible says about covenant and
    justice / Lois Barrett.
          p. cm.
    Bibliography: p.
    ISBN 0-8361-3490-7 (pbk.)
    1. Christianity and justice—Biblical teaching.   2. Covenants
(Theology)—Biblical teaching.   3. Bible—Study.   I. Title.
BR115.J8B37 1989
241'.62—dc19   88-22595
                                                                           CIP

The paper used in this publication meets the minimum requirements of
American National Standard for Information Sciences—Permanence of Paper for
Printed Library Materials, ANSI Z39.48-1984.

Mennonite Central Committee cover photo by Dennis Zehr.

Unless otherwise indicated, Scripture references are from the *Good
News Bible.* Old Testament copyright © American Bible Society 1976;
New Testament copyright © American Bible Society 1966, 1971, 1976.

Scripture references marked NIV are from the HOLY BIBLE: NEW
INTERNATIONAL VERSION. Copyright © 1973, 1978, 1984 by the
International Bible Society. Used by permission of Zondervan Bible
Publishers.

Scripture references marked RSV are from the Revised Standard Version
of the Bible, copyrighted 1946, 1952, © 1971, 1973.

To Mennonite Church of the Servant

Contents

*What does the Lord require of you
but to do justice, and to love kindness,
and to walk humbly with your God?*
—Micah 6:8, RSV

Foreword

Charles Dickens, author of *Oliver Twist*, tells how young children were forced to work long hours in the factories of England during the Industrial Revolution. Many of them became ill and some died of overwork and physical abuse.

The news media of our day often report stories of abuse and injustice. We hear of unfair prices for rents, of people being forced from their land by governments or large corporations. We read about large profits on food, clothing, and medicine, of meager wages for unskilled workers. We even hear of injustices because of skin color or corrupt systems of government.

Since injustice afflicts people around the world, how can we work for greater justice? Can we even agree on a definition of justice? More important, what does justice mean in everyday life? And what might God's plan for right relationships look like?

In *Doing What Is Right*, author Lois Barrett examines these kinds of questions. She observes that our common understandings of justice often have more to do with punishment for the evildoer than right relationships for all.

Rather than working to rebuild right relationships, the government's justice sends the evildoer to jail.

"The Bible speaks of a different kind of justice," she writes. "Biblical justice does not favor the rich. Nor does it even try to treat everyone the same. It goes beyond that, because it has a special concern for the poor and oppressed."

The author explores how God's kind of justice is different from justice as we usually know it. God's justice means living in a covenant relationship with the Creator and doing what is right for self and others. She observes how justice becomes the basis for true worship and how it leads to mercy and healing for the oppressed. Justice, of course, becomes judgment for the oppressor, too. Biblical justice often comes with a price, and she illustrates this from the life of Jesus and the early church.

The author's biblical treatment of justice is both insightful and inspiring. Her book is volume seven in a series on peace and justice themes listed near the back. It was commissioned by Mennonite Board of Missions, Mennonite Publishing House, the Peace Section of the Board of Congregational Ministries, and Mennonite Central Committee—all Mennonite agencies.

The series bridges the gap between scholarly Mennonite writings and narrowly focused evangelical literature that often neglects the social dimensions of the gospel. For further reading on the theme, check the sources listed near the end of the book.

—J. Allen Brubaker, Editor
Peace and Justice Series

CHAPTER 1

Real Justice

On top of the courthouse in my city stands a statue of justice. As in much of the Western world, here also justice is pictured as a woman holding scales. The scales are a symbol of each person getting his or her equal weight according to the law. In most of these statues, justice is blindfolded so she can judge objectively. That is, she judges not on the basis of her relationship to either person, but as if she did not know them.

That is the idea of justice that many people have. They think of the courts of law as just or fair when they treat everyone the same. So, a fair judge gives the same penalty for the same crime committed under the same circumstances, no matter who committed the crime. Justice means that each person gets what he or she deserves.

In this kind of justice, it is important that people who do wrong are punished, and people who are innocent go free. Punishment is more important than seeing that people are in right relationship with each other. For example, if someone steals from me, the government's justice may send that person to jail, but I am unlikely to get back what that person stole from me. Neither am I likely to be able to talk to the person who stole and see what could make it right between us. The purpose of the government's justice is to see that the guilty person is punished.

That kind of justice is a real improvement over law enforcement that favors the rich or the "important" people. We do not want judges or police officers who demand a bribe before they will judge in a person's favor. We think it is unfair when only poor people get harsh punishments and the rich get light sentences or no punishment at all.

The Bible speaks of a different kind of justice. Biblical justice does not favor the rich. Nor does it even try to treat everyone the same. It goes beyond that, because it has a special concern for the poor and oppressed. Psalm 72 is an ancient song of the people of Israel about what makes a good and just ruler:

Teach the king to judge with your righteousness, O God;
       share with him your own justice,
so that he will rule over your people with justice
       and govern the oppressed with righteousness.

May the land enjoy prosperity;
       may it experience righteousness.
May the king judge the poor fairly;
       may he help the needy and defeat their oppressors.
May your people worship you as long as the sun shines,
       as long as the moon gives light, for ages to come.

May the king be like rain on the fields,
       like showers falling on the land.
May righteousness flourish in his lifetime,

and may prosperity last as long as the moon gives
    light. . . .

He [the ruler] rescues the poor who call to him,
    and those who are needy and neglected.
He has pity on the weak and the poor;
    he saves the lives of those in need.
He rescues them from oppression and violence;
    their lives are precious to him. (Psalm 72:1-7, 12-14)

The ideal ruler in this psalm is one who takes a special interest in the poor, the weak, and the oppressed. The ruler does this because that is the kind of justice, or righteousness, that God shows to people. In this psalm, the people are asking God to give the ruler a sense of God's justice. God's justice is justice with a bias—a bent toward those who are in need. It is not equality for all, but special help for those with special needs. God's justice has a bias toward those people who count themselves as part of God's family and call on God for help. God's justice wants to set things right between people.

God's justice rescues a group of Hebrew slaves from Egypt and brings them into a land of plenty. God's justice gives victory to a small band armed only with torches, jars, and trumpets. God's justice brings the captives back from exile in Babylon. God's justice leaves the 99 sheep to search for the one who is lost. God's justice raises the crucified Jesus to life and glory. God's justice gives victory to the persecuted followers of the Lamb.

What kind of justice is this? Can we understand how God's justice is different from justice as we usually know and experience it?

CHAPTER 2

Living in
the Covenant

The Hebrew term used most often in the Old Testament for justice is *tsedek* (and other words which come from that root). Most older English versions of the Bible translate this word as "righteousness." But one can as well translate it "justice," as in many modern versions. We can also think of justice, or righteousness, as meaning "living in right relationship," or "being right with" someone.

The original life setting of the Hebrew word for justice is the covenant, or legal contract. Just as today, people in Bible times made contracts or covenants or agreements with each other. Jacob and Laban covenanted with each other by making a pile of stones. Jacob promised not to mistreat his wives, who were Laban's daughters. Both Jacob and Laban promised that they would not go past the pile of stones to harm the other. They put the covenant into effect by taking a vow, offering a sacrifice, and eating a meal together. (See Genesis 31:43-55.)

People were "righteous," or "just," concerning a covenant when they did what they had promised they would do. They were "just" (*tsadik*) if they kept the terms of the covenant. They were "unjust" or "unrighteous" if they did not live up to the covenant. Often, the people making the covenant called on God as a witness. For example, Laban said to Jacob, "May the Lord [Yahweh] keep an eye on us while we are separated from each other" (Genesis 31:49). Sacrifice of an animal appears to have been a way to say, "May God do to me as I have done to this animal, if I do not act as I have promised in this covenant."

We see how seriously people took a covenant when we read the story of David and Saul. David had a chance to kill King Saul when the king wanted to kill him. Instead of killing Saul, David cut off only a piece of Saul's clothing. He did this because of the covenant he and the people of Israel had made with Saul as their king. Even though Saul was his enemy, David did not harm him. Afterward, Saul told David, "You are more righteous than I. . . . You have treated me well, but I have treated you badly" (1 Samuel 24:17, NIV). In other words, David was righteous because he had lived up to his part of the covenant, but Saul had not.

The purpose of a covenant is to bring people into relationship with each other. Probably the first covenants were those that created a family relationship, such as marriage or adoption. For example, a parent adopting a child might make a covenant, saying, "From now on, I will be your father, and you will be my son." God's covenant with King David (Psalm 89:3) appears as a father/son adoption.

> He will say to me,
> "You are my father and my God;
>   you are my protector and savior."

I will make him my first-born son,
>   the greatest of all kings.
I will always keep my promise to him,
>   and my covenant with him will last forever.

God's covenant with people in the Old Testament are patterned after these family covenants. In some parts of the Old Testament, God's covenant with the people of Israel is like an adoption covenant, with Israel as God's child (Hosea 11). Or God's covenant with Israel is like a marriage covenant (Hosea 1—3). In that passage, worshiping other gods is like being unfaithful to one's husband. It is breaking the covenant.

Hosea and Gomer were married in Israel in the eighth century before the Christian era. The high point of their marriage ceremony was their saying, "You are now my wife, and I am now your husband." "You are now my husband, and I am now your wife." That was their marriage covenant.

The marriage did not go smoothly. In spite of bearing Hosea three children, Gomer was unfaithful to him. So Hosea did what he as a Hebrew husband had the right to do. He called together the elders of the town in front of the town gate (the court of law, in those days). He brought suit for divorce on ground of Gomer's adultery. He declared in public, "She is not my wife, and I am not her husband."

He not only sent her out of his house for public humiliation, he asked that her bride price be taken away from her. At the time of the engagement, the groom paid the bride price to the bride and her father as a kind of insurance policy. It protected the woman against poverty in case her husband died or decided to divorce her. The husband could ask for the bride price back only if the wife committed adultery.

That was what Hosea did. He asked for the vineyards and orchards and the other things he had given to Gomer.

After that, Hosea did a strange thing. He went courting Gomer again. He told her he wanted a new covenant with her. He told her that if she would stop sleeping around with other men and be faithful to him, he wanted her back. He asked her to make with him a covenant of righteousness and justice, of steadfast love and mercy.

Gomer said yes. So Hosea paid a new bride price of silver and barley and married her again. And the new covenant, the new relationship began.

Hosea did not hide the story of his up-and-down marriage. He told it publicly. He said that Israel's relationship with God was like Gomer's relationship with Hosea. Israel had broken its covenant with God. Israel had been worshiping other gods. So God would allow Israel to reap the consequences of its sin. But God wanted a new covenant with a faithful Israel: a covenant of righteousness and justice, of steadfast love and mercy. God said, "You are now my people, and I am your God." That was God's kind of justice.

Covenant is the context for understanding much of the faith language of the Bible. The word *faith* itself is a part of covenant language. In the noun form, it usually means "faithfulness." In the verb forms, it often means "to be faithful" or "to believe." It means to trust in someone else's faithfulness to a covenant. In any covenant relationship, faithfulness involves not only committing oneself fully to the relationship. It also means giving up suspicion that the other may not be fully committed.

Genesis 15:6 says, concerning God's covenant with Abram, that "Abram believed [had faith in] the LORD, and he credited it to him as righteousness [justice]" (NIV). In other words, Abram accepted the covenant that God offered. He trusted that God would keep God's promises and he committed himself to living by that covenant. So, God counted Abram as just, or righteous, as living in right relationship with the one who had made the covenant.

To have faith in God, then, means to be faithful to God and to the covenant we have made with God. To have faith in God also means trusting that God will continue to be faithful to us.

God's covenant with the people of Israel was not an impersonal contract. It was a covenant to become family. The covenant was held together by *steadfast love*. This word is sometimes translated *loving-kindness*, or *mercy*. This is love that goes beyond just keeping the rules. When a husband shows steadfast love to his wife, he does extra favors for her. He does more for her than that required by any agreements they have made. Instead, he does what will help their relationship to continue.

In this way, God showed steadfast love toward Israel (Psalm 32:10). Likewise, Israel was to show steadfast love toward God (Hosea 6:4). A covenant holds together when both persons show mercy toward each other. They go more than halfway to meet each other. Their love for each other is willing to overlook the small irritations so they can continue to be in relationship with each other.

This steadfast love is related to several other words: *grace, compassion, faithfulness,* and *forgiveness*. All these ideas appear in God's revelation to Moses in Exodus 34:5-7a.

> Then the LORD came down in the cloud and stood there with him [Moses] and proclaimed his name, the LORD [Yahweh]. And he passed in front of Moses, proclaiming, "The LORD, the LORD, the compassionate and gracious God, slow to anger, abounding in love and faithfulness, maintaining love to thousands, and forgiving wickedness, rebellion, and sin."   (NIV)

These are traits of God that make it possible for human beings to live in covenant with God. People do rebel against God's covenant. They sin. But when they repent, God is eager to *forgive*. God does not count their sin against them. God has *compassion* on those who do not deserve it.

The Hebrew word for "compassion" comes from the word which means "womb." So the compassion of God for those adopted into God's family through the covenant is like the compassion of a mother for the child born from her womb. God is *gracious*. God does favors for those who are part of the covenant.

Because God is like this, when God's people are in trouble, God saves them. The writer of Psalm 6 prays, "Come and save me, LORD; in your mercy rescue me from death" (verse 4). The people of God expect to be saved from their enemies because they have made a covenant with God. God is their most powerful "next-of-kin." So God is responsible to save them.

These ideas tell about what happens to bring about justice when things are going well. But what if people broke their covenant? What if they had promised to give back the plow they had borrowed, but they did not, and the owner of the plow accused them of stealing?

The Hebrew language has a second word for justice:

mishpat. If justice as *tsedek* is a general "living in right relationship" with someone, justice as *mishpat* is more specific. *Mishpat* is deciding what is "just" when two people disagree or when one has hurt the other.

Mishpat was decided in the court of law at the gate of an Israelite town. In early Israel and even during the time of the kings, most legal conflicts were settled at the town gate.

At the gate to a walled town was a large open space. Sometimes stone seats were built into the opening in the wall. On their way out to the fields to work in the morning, the heads of households in the town gathered here. If two people had a dispute, they called together the town elders. The elders listened to both sides of the dispute. Then they gave a judgment (*mishpat*) on who was in the right (*tsedek*) and who was in the wrong and how to right the wrong. (See Ruth 4:1-12.)

If the dispute could not be settled at the town gate, in the time of early Israel, one could take the dispute to a "judge." For example, Deborah served as a judge. She sat under a palm tree between the towns of Ramah and Bethel. The people of Israel would go there for her decisions (Judges 4:4-5).

A judge was to give a decision that would give justice to the one who had been offended or oppressed. That might mean some punishment for the offender. But the goal was to restore right relationships within the community. Through his or her judgments, the judge brought justice back to the community.

The judge was also responsible to bring justice between Israel and other nations. Deborah as judge called for Barak to stop the cruelty and violence of Jabin, a Canaanite king, toward the people of Israel (Judges 4). Gideon as judge brought justice to Israel by driving out the Midianites (Judges 6—8). So wherever God's people were oppressed, a judge was called to bring justice, to restore right relationships.

After Israel had kings, the kings took over both these roles of the judges. They brought justice between individuals in the kingdom by judging in disputes, as in a court of law. And they brought justice between nations, by rescuing Israel from nations that oppressed them.

The Old Testament also speaks of God as a judge. As judge, God can make a just decision (*mishpat*) for someone who is harassed by oppressors. Psalm 35 says,

> Rouse yourself, O Lord, and defend me;
>   rise up, my God, and plead my cause.
> You are righteous, O LORD, so declare me innocent;
>   don't let my enemies gloat over me.   (vv. 23-24)
>
> May those who want to see me acquitted
>   shout for joy and say again and again,
> "How great is the LORD!
>   He is pleased with the success of his servant."
>
> Then I will proclaim your righteousness,
>   and I will praise you all day long.   (vv. 27-28)

Part of the righteousness (justice) of God is that God as judge declares as innocent the one who has been oppressed.

God is also judge in that God defends Israel from national enemies. Psalm 7:8 declares that God is the judge of all humankind. Not only Israel, but all the nations should live according to God's justice. Otherwise, the judgments of God may go against them. God, says the psalm, saves those who obey God.

On the one hand, God raises up the righteous, those who live according to God's covenant. On the other hand, God puts down the wicked, those who are oppressing others. This other side of God's justice is God's wrath, or anger. People see the wrath of God when God gives over wicked people to be caught in their own evil. Psalm 7 continues:

> See how wicked people think up evil;
> > they plan trouble and practice deception.
> But in the traps they set for others,
> > they themselves get caught.

> So they are punished by their own evil
> > and are hurt by their own violence.
> I thank the LORD for his justice;
> > I sing praises to the LORD, the Most High.
>
> > > > > > > (vv. 14-17)

Or people experience the wrath of God when they sin and experience the absence of God (Psalm 89:46).

So God as judge acts both to defend the righteous (those who are right with the covenant) and condemn those who act against the covenant. Both actions are part of God's salvation. All God's acts of judgment are the result of God's merciful love toward the righteous, the poor, and the oppressed. The prayer of Hannah celebrates the justice of God.

> [God] lifts the poor from the dust
> > and raises the needy from their misery.
> He makes them companions of princes

and puts them in places of honor.
The foundations of the earth belong to the LORD;
on them he has built the world.
He protects the lives of his faithful people,
but the wicked disappear in darkness;
A man does not triumph by his own strength.
The LORD's enemies will be destroyed;
He will thunder against them from heaven.
The LORD will judge the whole world.
(1 Samuel 2:8-10b)

The judgments of God for the oppressed and the needy bring justice for them and for the community. The purpose of covenant is to maintain right relationships within the community. When oppressors stop hurting the oppressed, the whole community can experience justice.

Another Hebrew word related to justice is *shalom*, often translated *peace*. It has to do with wholeness or completeness. When there is *shalom*, then there are right relationships within the community. *Shalom* is much more than just the absence of fighting. *Shalom* means good relationships marked by justice. Isaiah 32:16-17 shows the connection between peace and justice when the Spirit of God is poured out upon the people:

Justice [*mishpat*] will dwell in the desert
and righteousness [*tsedek*] live in the fertile field.
The fruit of righteousness will be peace [*shalom*];
the effect of righteousness will be quietness and
confidence forever.   (NIV)

Here, the outcome of justice is peace, right relationships, and security.

So, God is a God of justice. God lives up to the covenant that brings us into a family relationship. God wants people to act according to the covenant, too. Like a caring parent, God acts to keep family members from hurting each other, lifting the one who is hurt and stopping the offender from doing further harm. Like a caring parent, God is more interested in bringing people into right relationship with each other than in making sure they get all the punishment they deserve. Like a caring parent, God keeps reaching out toward people in love and mercy. That is God's kind of justice.

CHAPTER 3

The Direction of the Covenant

Imagine that you are an Israelite in 1100 B.C. You had worked hard at growing your crops, tending your vineyard and your trees, and taking care of your livestock. But sickness a few years go took your husband and three of your five children. Now you are widowed, with one son and one daughter. Life isn't easy, but it is possible. You gather grain at harvesttime from the corners of others' fields. (According to the law, harvesters are to leave those corners for the poor.)

At one point, you had to sell your son as a servant to a neighbor. However, thanks be to God, your brother-in-law was able to buy him back. You also had to sell the land of your husband's family. No relative has found the resources to buy back the land. At least the land will not be out of the family forever. In the Year of Jubilee, it will be returned to your descendants.

Now is the time of the third-year tithe. This tenth of all crops is given to the Levites, the foreigners, the orphans, and the widows so all will have enough to eat.

When the tithe is brought to the priests, each landowner will say to God,

> My ancestor was a wandering Aramean, who took his family to Egypt to live. They were few in number when they went there, but they became a large and powerful nation. The Egyptians treated us harshly and forced us to work as slaves. Then we cried out for help to the LORD, the God of our ancestors. He heard us and saw our suffering, hardship, and misery. By his great power and strength, he rescued us from Egypt. He worked miracles and wonders, and caused terrifying things to happen. He brought us here and gave us this rich and fertile land. So now I bring to the LORD the first part of the harvest that he has given me. . . .

> None of the sacred tithe is left in my house; I have given it to the Levites, the foreigners, the orphans, and the widows, as you commanded me to do. I have not disobeyed or forgotten any of your commands concerning the tithe. . . . I have obeyed you, O LORD; I have done everything you commanded concerning the tithe. Look down from your holy place in heaven and bless your people Israel; bless also the rich and fertile land that you have given us, as you promised our ancestors.   (Adapted from Deuteronomy 26)

You know that God has promised that if you obey all God's laws with all your heart, God calls you his people. You say, "You are my God, so I obey your law." God says, "You are my own people. I will be faithful to you."

So you pray a prayer of thanks to God for the law. The law protects you. The law gives you food and shelter. The law preserves you and your family within the community. The law is the mercy of God toward you, a widow.

What the people of God were to do to live in the covenant was set forth in the *torah*. *Torah* is usually translated *law*. But that is not the best way of looking at *torah*. Actually, the Hebrew word means "direction," or "teaching." The word appears as a verb in Genesis 46:28, where Judah goes ahead of the rest of the family "to point out" the way to Goshen. This is what law, or *torah*, is to do: to point out the direction in which the people of God should go.

This is quite different from the way we usually see "law." We usually look at law as a set of rules. Rules say what to do and, most often, what not to do. One can do exactly what the rules say, no more, no less, but still not live according to the intention of the one who made the rules. In English idiom, we call this "following the letter of the law."

The Bible, however, tells us to live according to the spirit of the law. The Hebrew word for "commandment" suggests not just an order, but also a pile of stones that served as a signpost or guidepost. Even what we call the Ten Commandments are not worded as commands. Instead, the verbs are in a tense that implies this is the way things are, or this is the way things will be. So instead of "You shall not steal," Exodus 20:15 means, "[If you want to live justly in the community of the people of God] you will not be stealing."

Apparently this is indeed how the people of early Israel saw the law. Take, for example, the story of King David and the woman of Tekoa found in 2 Samuel 14. This woman went to the king for judgment concerning her son. She was a widow who had had two sons. They quarreled, and one killed the other. Her relatives were now demand-

ing that she follow the law and turn the remaining son over
to them. Then they would kill him as his punishment
under the law. But then, she complained, there would be
no man in the family to support her. She said,

> "Your Majesty, please pray to the LORD your God, so that
> my relative who is responsible for avenging the death of my
> son will not commit a greater crime by killing my other
> son."

> "I promise by the living LORD," David replied, "that your
> son will not be harmed in the least."   (2 Samuel 14:11)

The letter of the law was to kill the person who had murdered. The spirit of the law was to do what would bring
back right relationships (justice) to the community. There
would have been no justice if the widow had been left in
poverty with no son to support her. The collections of laws
were not so much rules to enforce, but testimony to the justice God wanted within the community of Israel.

Later King Josiah found the books of the Law after they
had been lost. The changes he made at that time may have
been the beginning of the idea that the law of God was the
same as the written words. This idea continued when Ezra
and Nehemiah brought some of the Jewish exiles back
from Babylon. They set up a new Jewish community
around Jerusalem. This community was to govern itself by
the written law.

Yet, even after Josiah, some of the prophets had the idea
of the true law as a law written upon the heart (Jeremiah
31:33). The law of the heart did not need a written law
covering every possible crime. The law of the heart was the
gift of God. It was a gift of grace because it gave people the

direction they needed to live in justice within the covenant.

The Old Testament connects the giving of the law (*torah*) with the making of the covenant at Mount Sinai. (Sinai is called "Horeb" in the book of Deuteronomy.) Exodus 20:2 also connects the basis of the law with the realization that God is the one "who brought you out of Egypt, where you were slaves." Throughout the law are reminders that God had saved the Hebrew people from slavery in Egypt. Then, through the covenant, God made them a nation. This is the kind of God who gives the law, a God who hears the cry of the poor and the oppressed and rescues them. Exodus 2:23-25 says:

> Years later the king of Egypt died, but the Israelites were still groaning under their slavery and cried out for help. Their cry went up to God, who heard their groaning and remembered his covenant with Abraham, Isaac, and Jacob. He saw the slavery of the Israelites and was concerned.

So the law reflects the concern of God for the oppressed and for all who cry for help. God chose the people of Israel not because they were such a large nation (Deuteronomy 7:7-8). God made a covenant with them because they cried to God for help. God was concerned for justice for them. God wanted to set things right.

Because God had saved them out of oppression, the people of Israel were also to have special concern for the poor. Deuteronomy 10:17-19 states: The LORD your God is supreme over all gods and over all powers.

> He is great and mighty, and he is to be obeyed. He does not show partiality, and he does not accept bribes. He makes

sure that orphans and widows are treated fairly; he loves the foreigners who live with our people, and gives them food and clothes. So then, show love for those foreigners, because you were once foreigners in Egypt.

Some of the laws are "case laws." That means that they grew out of the cases brought before the elders at the town gate.

For example, Exodus 22:1 states, "If a man steals a cow or a sheep and kills it or sells it, he must pay five cows for one cow and four sheep for one sheep." This form of law is familiar throughout the law codes of other nations in the ancient Near East. It states the situation, "if . . . " and the penalty, "then . . . ."

What is special about biblical law (especially in Leviticus and Deuteronomy) are statements with a "motive clause." In these laws, the command comes first, then a motive or reason for obeying the command. For example, Leviticus 19:33-34 says,

> Do not mistreat foreigners who are living in your land. Treat them as you would a fellow Israelite, and love them as you love yourselves. Remember that you were once foreigners in the land of Egypt. I am the LORD [Yahweh] your God.

Or consider Deuteronomy 24:17-18:

> Do not deprive foreigners and orphans of their rights; and do not take a widow's garment as security for a loan. Remember that you were slaves in Egypt and that the LORD [Yahweh] set you free; that is why I have given you this command.

Or people were to bring a tenth of their crops as harvest offerings. This tithe was for the ministers at the altars, the foreigners, the orphans, and the widows. The reason for bringing these offerings was that God had heard the cry of the Israelites, rescued them from Egypt, and brought them into a rich and fertile land. So now they were to share their crops with those who did not have their own land to farm. (See Deuteronomy 16:1-15.)

These laws with "motive clauses" show the main direction of the law. The justice of God was the mercy that paid special attention to the oppressed and the needy. The justice of God set things right between person and person and between person and God. So the justice practiced by the people of God was also to bring the oppressed and the needy into full community.

This justice appears especially in the Sabbath and Jubilee laws. (See Leviticus 25 and Exodus 23:10-12.) Every seventh day was a day of rest, not only for householders, but for servants and foreigners employed by the householders. Every seventh year was a year of rest so the poor could harvest the volunteer crop. Every fiftieth year (seven times seven plus one) was a Jubilee year. During that year, any family property that had been sold was returned to the original family. All were to set their slaves free. They were to forgive their loans. Following the direction of these laws meant there could be no permanent upper and lower classes. Every 50 years, equality would be restored.

Digging at the sites of ancient Israelite villages shows that this was indeed the case in early Israel before the time of the kings. During that period, all the houses were about the same size and with the same kinds of utensils.

However, digging at the levels of later periods, during the time of the kings, shows that upper and lower classes did develop as kings neglected to declare Jubilee years.

So the intent of the Sabbath and Jubilee laws was to create and maintain a community in which there was economic justice.

Even the holiness laws (see the book of Leviticus) guided the people toward keeping a community in right relationship with each other and God. These laws were about religious celebrations and right worship, about what to eat and what sexual practices were forbidden, about how to treat contagious diseases, and about how to care for the poor. They were all directed at maintaining a community that was "clean" before God. Anything unclean was sent away so nothing would come between the person and God, or between the person and another person. That is justice, because the "clean" community experiences peace and wholeness.

So the law, the *torah*, was not a burdensome set of rules. Following *torah* was not a chore. *Torah* was a gift from God. *Torah* gave direction on how to stay living within the covenant God had made with the people of Israel. *Torah* was a guide to staying in right relationship with God and with other people.

Those who followed the way in which *torah* directed them were the righteous. They were the ones who practiced justice. They were righteous because they had been faithful to the way of the covenant. They had shown mercy to the needy, as God had shown mercy to them and their ancestors. They thanked God for giving them *torah* because it showed them the way to justice and peace. This is why Psalm 119 sings out its praise of the law:

How I love your law [*torah*]!
>I think about it all day long.
Your commandment is with me all the time
>and makes me wiser than my enemies.

I understand more than all my teachers,
>because I meditate on your instructions.
I have greater wisdom than old men,
>because I obey your commands.

I have avoided all evil conduct,
>because I want to obey your word.
I have not neglected your instructions [words of justice],
>because you yourself are my teacher [the one who
>shows me *torah*].

How sweet is the taste of your instructions—
>sweeter even than honey!
I gain wisdom from your laws,
>and so I hate all bad conduct.   (vv. 97-104)

God had been faithful to them by saving them from their enemies, as God had promised through the covenant. Through the gift of the law, they saw the justice of God even more. Through the law, God gave the people of Israel direction on how they also could be faithful to the covenant. To follow that direction meant righteousness and justice.

CHAPTER 4

Worship and Justice

The books of the Law are not the only part of the Old Testament to speak about justice. The Prophets and the Writings (especially the Psalms) are full of justice language. Both the Prophets and the Writings are clear that only the righteous (the just) can truly worship God. Only those who do justice have the right to call on God to do justice for them.

The Psalms were the worship book of the people of Israel. How important justice was in their worship! All the language of covenant justice is there in the Psalms. The word for *justice/righteousness* (*tsedek*, in its various forms) appears 137 times in the Psalms. *Mercy/steadfast love/loving-kindness* appears 120 times; *judge*, 27 times; and *justice/judgment* (*mishpat*), 65 times. *Faithfulness* appears 22 times; *covenant*, 21 times; *to save* or *salvation*, 76 times; *to deliver*, 45 times; and *peace*, 27 times.

There are three types of psalms. The first is the psalm of praise. These psalms tell how great God is because God has been faithful to what God promised in the covenant and has saved the people from their trouble. Most of the time these psalms do not say just, "Praise the Lord." They say why they are praising the Lord. They say what God did to create justice. They thank God for restoring right relationships, peace, or health. Psalm 147 is such a praise psalm.

> Praise the LORD [Yahweh]!
>
> It is good to sing praise to our God;
>   it is pleasant and right to praise him.
> The LORD is restoring Jerusalem;
>   he is bringing back the exiles.
> He heals the broken-hearted
>   and bandages their wounds.   (vv. 1-3)

The second type is the psalm that teaches what people must do to stay in right relationship with God. Psalm 1 is like this.

> Happy are those who reject the advice of evil [people],
>   who do not follow the example of sinners
>   or join those who have no use for God.
> Instead, they find joy in obeying the Law of the LORD,
>   and they study it day and night.   (vv. 1-2)

The third type is the psalm of lament. This is really a psalm of complaining. These psalms cry out to God to save the people from the trouble that they are in now. Most of the psalms are laments. Psalm 7 is typical.

> O LORD [Yahweh], my God, I come to you for protection;
>   rescue me and save me from all who pursue me . . . .
> Rise in your anger, O LORD!

Stand up against the fury of my enemies;
rouse yourself and help me!

Justice is what you demand,
so bring together all the peoples around you,
and rule over them from above.
You are the judge of all [peoples].
Judge in my favor, O LORD;
you know that I am innocent.
You are a righteous God
and judge our thoughts and desires.
Stop the wickedness of evil [people]
and reward those who are good.   (vv. 1,6-9)

Usually, these psalms of lament remind God of how God has been faithful in the past, bringing justice, rescuing those who keep the covenant, and bringing disaster on those who break the covenant. Then the psalms tell how bad things are now. They tell how much others are trying to hurt them. Now, say these psalms, because we know you are a just God, bring justice for us again. Then we will praise you in front of the congregation and tell everyone of your justice. (See Psalms 35:28; 52:9.)

The psalms give us a picture of worship that includes not only praise, confession, and teaching, but cries for help. Those who pray the psalms are those who have experienced trouble (sickness, sin, war, oppression, poverty). Then they cry to God. They expect that the God who has made a covenant with them will be faithful and keep that covenant. If they also are faithful to the covenant, God will hear their cry and save them from their trouble. That is the way God's loving mercy works. Psalm 146 says with confidence:

> [Yahweh] always keeps his promises;
> > he judges in favor of the oppressed
> > and gives food to the hungry.
> The LORD sets prisoners free
> > and gives sight to the blind.
>
> He lifts those who have fallen;
> > he loves his righteous people.
> He protects the strangers who live in our land;
> > he helps widows and orphans,
> > but takes the wicked to their ruin.
>
> The LORD is king forever.
> Your God, O Zion, will reign for all time.
> Praise the LORD!   (vv. 6b-10)

But what happened if the people of God were not faithful to the covenant? What if they did not do justice? Then God would bring a lawsuit against them.

In the Prophets, we find several examples of God taking the people of Israel to court. In Isaiah 1:2-31, God calls earth and sky as witnesses to the sins of Israel. God is disgusted with all their worship rituals because they are corrupted by their sins. God will ignore their hands lifted in prayer because their hands are covered with blood. They must "stop doing evil and learn to do right. They must do justice—help those who are oppressed, give orphans their rights, and defend widows" (vv. 16b-17). God charges that the leaders of Israel take bribes. They never defend orphans in court or listen when widows present their case (v. 23).

Those who do not repent will wither like a garden that no one waters. As straw is set on fire by a spark, so their own evil deeds will destroy the powerful.

Even in this lawsuit God shows the mercy in God's justice. Because God is a God of justice, God will save everyone in Jerusalem who repents. God is willing to settle the matter by washing the bloodstains from their hands and making them "clean." When they are clean, then they are part of the covenant community again. Then they can offer right worship to God again. In this lawsuit, God is prosecutor, judge, plaintiff, and the one who offers mercy.

Other lawsuits appear throughout the writings of the prophets. In Isaiah 3:13-15, God states the case against those who take advantage of the poor. The lawsuit in Isaiah 5 compares the people of Jerusalem and Judah to a vineyard that produced sour grapes. Their offenses are that they committed murder and injustice. Hosea 1—3 accuses Israel of unfaithfulness by worshiping other gods. Hosea 4 accuses Israel of breaking promises, lying, murder, stealing, adultery, and worshiping fertility gods.

Amos 5 states the case against those who keep the poor from getting justice in the courts. God hates religious festivals and sacrifices and songs, says Amos, when they are offered by those who do not practice justice. "Instead, let justice flow like a stream, and righteousness like a river that never goes dry" (v. 24).

In Micah 6 the lawsuit against the people of Israel finds a more complete form. First, the prophet calls the mountains and the hills as witnesses. Then God reminds the people of all God has done in the past to save them: bringing them out of Egypt, sending Moses, Aaron, and Miriam to lead them. Then the prophet tells what God requires for right worship. Sacrifices are not so important. Rather, what the Lord requires is "to do what is just, to

show constant love, and to live in humble fellowship with
our God" (v. 8).

God then lists the crimes of the people: using false
weights and measures, exploiting the poor, and gaining
wealth dishonestly. The punishments for these sins are
then listed. They will eat but never be satisfied. They will
have their belongings destroyed in war. They will plant
crops but not be able to harvest them. They will be looked
down on by others. But chapter seven ends with the
prophet telling of the mercy of God. God will forgive the
sins of the people who survive. God will be faithful to the
covenant made with their ancestors and will be merciful
again.

By the time of the prophets and kings, Israelite society
had come to have upper and lower classes. There was no
longer equality among the people. Kings drafted men into
military service instead of having all-volunteer armies. The
poor were not always treated with the concern that the law
required. Those who worked in the temple became part of
the power structure around the king and the upper classes.
Even the temple did not always stand for justice.

The intent of sacrifices in the tabernacle (or later in the
temple) was to bring the person offering the sacrifice back
into right relationship in covenant with God. Those offering sacrifices placed their hands on the sacrifice as a way of
identifying themselves with the sacrifice. In this way, they
showed publicly that they were repenting of their sin. Or
they thanked God for healing them or saving them in some
other way. Or they committed themselves again to the
covenant. Sacrifice meant commitment to justice, to living
in right relationship.

The prophets knew that religious activities alone did not

keep people in right relationship with God and the covenant. Of what use were sacrifices or fasting if people did not commit themselves to living justly? The fasting God wants, says Isaiah 58:6-9, is this:

> Remove the chains of oppression and the yoke of injustice, and let the oppressed go free. Share your food with the hungry and open your homes to the homeless poor. Give clothes to those who have nothing to wear, and do not refuse to help your own relatives. Then my favor will shine on you like the morning sun, and your wounds will be quickly healed. I will always be with you to save you; my presence will protect you on every side. When you pray, I will answer you. When you call to me, I will respond.

In order to keep a right relationship with God, the people had to be in right relationship with their neighbors. They needed to act with merciful justice toward the poor and the weak, as God acted with merciful justice toward them. There could be no *shalom*, no health and peace and wholeness, in the covenant community when the poor and weak were oppressed.

If people oppressed the poor, the justice of God meant punishment for their sin. If people treated the poor with mercy, then they could ask for the mercy of God in their prayers and hymns and sacrifices. The best sacrifices were joined with doing justice, loving with mercy, and having a humble relationship with God.

Imagine coming to the temple in Jerusalem in the eighth century B.C. You are wealthy. You are bringing a sheep for a sacrifice. As you enter temple courts, you see a crowd gathered around a man who is singing. So you get a firmer hold on the rope around your sheep and stop to listen.

> My friend had a vineyard on a very fertile hill.
> He dug the soil and cleared it of stones;
> He planted the finest vines.
> He built a tower to guard them,
> Dug a pit for treading the grapes.
> He waited for the grapes to ripen,
> But every grape was—
> Sour!

The crowed murmured sympathetically. Then the singer began talking, "Well, now, folks. Who was in the right— my vineyard or I? Is there anything I failed to do for it?"

"No, no," we said.

"Then why didn't it produce good grapes?" he shouted. "Let me tell you what I am going to do with my vineyard. I am going to tear down the wall around it and let the wild animals eat it and trample it. I will quit hoeing it. I will let the weeds grow. I will even forbid the clouds to rain on it!"

Chuckles came from the crowd. Was this a joke? Was he a little crazy, or just very angry? The singer began the second verse:

> Israel is the vineyard of the LORD of hosts.
> The people of Judah are the vines he planted.
> God looked for right judgment,
> But saw bloodshed.
> God looked for right relationships,
> But heard the cries for justice.

The crowd shifted uncomfortably as the singer now spoke, "You are the vineyard that yielded sour grapes. You are the vineyard that God will tear down. You keep buying more houses and fields to add to those you already have.

You push out the poor, the widows, the orphans. Soon you will be living alone in the land.

> But you will pay for the injustices you have done. Those vineyards you have are going to quit producing for you. Those fine houses are going to be empty. You will no longer feast, but will go hungry. You will be carried away as prisoners. A distant nation will come like a whirlwind to defeat you in that day. The land will see only darkness and distress.
>
> Those sacrifices you are bringing to the temple will not get you on the right side of God, unless you stop doing evil. If you want to be in right relationship with God, then quit buying up the land of the poor. Help the oppressed. Give orphans their rights. Defend the widows. Then God will cleanse you and wash away your sin.
>
> (Adapted from Isaiah 5 and 1)

You look at the sheep tugging gently on the rope. You think about the land you bought last month from the widow of Eleazar. What is right? Should you go ahead and offer the sacrifice you have brought? What is the connection between worship and justice?

CHAPTER 5

The Task of the Servant of Yahweh

Tomorrow is the Sabbath. As leader of a Jewish synagogue in Babylon you are responsible tomorrow to give a teaching during the service. It is hard knowing what to say to your people. They have been taken by force from their homeland to Babylon. They are a people who have suffered military defeat. They do not know when, if ever, they will be allowed to return home. Here, among their captors, they try to work and pray and keep the Law and even sing.

It is not right, you think, that we should be in exile. It is not right that we should be captives. It is not right that we should be oppressed. It is not right that we should have to live among a people who do not understand us or our God.

But what can we do about it? A violent revolution would do no good. We are too few and too weak. We all would be killed. It is not possible to sneak out of the country and back home over the long distances. What is left? Passive acceptance of our situation? No. God has promised to be faithful to us. God has promised to bring justice for us.

You pray, "God, you are our God, and we are your people. Remember now your covenant with our ancestors and with us. Help us. Save us. Deliver us from the land of exile. Let your justice be established in all the world!"

But how will God's justice come? Then you remember what the prophet has written.

> Here is my servant, whom I strengthen—
> The one I have chosen, with whom I am pleased.
> I have filled him with my spirit,
> And he will bring justice to every nation.
>
> He will not shout or raise his voice
> Or make loud speeches in the streets.
> He will not break off a bent reed
> Nor put out a flickering lamp.
>
> He will bring lasting justice to all.
> He will not lose hope or courage;
> He will establish justice on the earth.
> Distant lands eagerly wait for his teaching [torah].

That will be your text tomorrow (adapted from Isaiah 42).

God promises blessing for those who do justice and punishment for those who turn justice away. Sometimes this does not happen right away. Why do blessings for those who do justice not always come now? Why do the righteous suffer? What is God going to do about it?

These are the questions of the book of Job. Job was a righteous man, yet he suffered. Job remained right with God because he had faith that God would bring justice in the end. But the only answer God gave Job to his why question was, "Who are you to question my wisdom?... Were you there when I made the world?" (Job 38:2, 4).

A clearer answer comes from the prophets, especially from the songs about the Servant of Yahweh, found in Isaiah 40—66. These songs grew out of the suffering of the people of Israel.

In 722 B.C. the armies of Assyria defeated Samaria, the capital city of Israel, the Northern Kingdom. About 150 years later, Jerusalem, the capital of Judah, the Southern Kingdom, was defeated. Its leaders were exiled to Babylon. The prophets and those who followed the thinking of the book of Deuteronomy saw these defeats as punishment for the nation. They thought that God had allowed enemies to defeat them because they had not followed God's way of justice.

What about those people who had practiced justice? Had God rejected them? Were they no longer God's people? Isaiah 49:14-15 talks about this dilemma.

> But the people of Jerusalem said,
> "The LORD has abandoned us!
>   He has forgotten us."
>
> So the LORD answers,
> "Can a woman forget her own baby
>   and not love the child she bore?
>
> Even if a mother should forget her child,
>   I will never forget you."

God's people had been defeated. They had received the consequences of their not practicing justice. But God still remembered the covenant that God and Israel would be family to each other. God would be more faithful to Jerusalem than a mother to her baby. God still offered a covenant to those who followed God's way of justice.

Even if the present looked bleak, God would come in the future to save God's people, said the book of Isaiah. God would remember the covenant to bring justice to the people when they were oppressed. Things may look bad now, but God will keep promises. The righteousness (justice) of God would become clear when God came to save the people. Isaiah 59:15-21 said that God is displeased that there is no justice.

> He is astonished to see that there is no one to help the oppressed. So he will use his own power to rescue them and to win the victory. He will wear justice like a coat of armor and saving power like a helmet. He will clothe himself with the strong desire to set things right and to punish and avenge the wrongs that people suffer. He will punish his enemies according to what they have done, even those who live in distant lands. From east to west everyone will fear him and his great power. He will come like a rushing river, like a strong wind.

> The LORD says to his people, "I will come to Jerusalem to defend you and to save all of you that turn from your sins. And I make a covenant with you: I have given you my power and my teachings to be yours forever, and from now on you are to obey me and teach your children and your descendants to obey me for all time to come."

Other prophets in this era after the defeat of Israel and Judah had a name for the time when God would save the covenant people. They called this time the "day of the Lord," or the "day of Yahweh." On that day, God would judge the whole earth and restore right relationships among people. The people of God would no longer be oppressed.

Then it would be clear to all the world that God alone was ruler. Then, God's justice would be established. The new king appointed by God would come riding in victory.

> Rejoice greatly, O Daughter of Zion!
>> Shout, daughter of Jerusalem!
>
> See, your king comes to you,
>> righteous [*tsadik*] and having salvation,
> gentle and riding on a donkey,
>> on a colt, the foal of a donkey.
>
> I will take away the chariots from Ephraim
>> and the war-horses from Jerusalem,
>> and the battle bow will be broken.
> He will proclaim peace to the nations.
>
> His rule will extend from sea to sea
>> and from the River to the ends of the earth.
> As for you, because of the blood of my covenant with you,
>> I will free your prisoners from the waterless pit. . . .
>
> Then the Lord will appear over them;
>> his arrow will flash like lightning.
> The Sovereign LORD will sound the trumpet. . . .
>
> The LORD their God will save them on that day
>> as the flock of his people.
> They will sparkle in his land
>> like jewels in a crown.

> (Zechariah 9:9-11, 14, 16, NIV)

The day of Yahweh would be a time of judgment. Then those who had been righteous concerning the covenant would know the salvation of God. But God would testify against "sorcerers, adulterers and perjurers, against those who defraud laborers of their wages, who oppress the widows and the fatherless, and deprive aliens of justice, but do not fear me" (Malachi 3:5, NIV). On the day of Yahweh, justice would be restored.

In spite of how bad things looked now, the people of God had hope that the justice of God would win in the end. One way that this would happen was through the Servant of Yahweh. The last half of the book of Isaiah includes many songs about this Servant. Sometimes the Servant seems to be the whole nation of Israel (Isaiah 41:8). Other times, the Servant seems to be one person.

This Servant of Yahweh acts through the Spirit of God. That is, God has chosen the Servant to bring about God's justice. Isaiah 61:1-3 outlines the mission of the Servant:

> The spirit of the Lord Yahweh is upon me
>> because Yahweh has anointed me.
> To bring good news to the poor, Yahweh has sent me,
>> to bind up those whose hearts are crushed,
>> to proclaim liberty to those taken captive,
> And to those imprisoned, opening,
>> to proclaim the year pleasing to Yahweh
>> and a day when our God will set right what is
>> wrong;
>> to comfort all mourners,
>> to give to the mourners of Zion,
>> to give to them a festive hat instead of ashes,
>> oil of joy instead of mourning,
>> a coat of glory instead of a spirit of belittlement.

> They will be called the oaks of justice,
>> planted by Yahweh so that people may give glory to
>> Yahweh.   (Author's translation)

The Servant will bring about God's justice gently, without violence, persistently. The Servant will continue to do this until justice comes to all people. Then *torah*, God's direction to people so they can live in justice, will be available to everyone (Isaiah 42:1-4).

Before their defeat, the people of Israel had understood that God's way meant practicing justice within the covenant community. Being right with God meant doing justice toward the poor and the weak within their own nation.

But now, says Isaiah 49, that vision is too small. Now, the task of the Servant of God is to bring justice to all nations, even to the ends of the earth. Yahweh tells the Servant:

> It is too small a thing for you to be my servant
>> to restore the tribes of Jacob
>> and to bring back those of Israel I have kept.
> I will also make you a light for the Gentiles [the nations].
>> that you may bring my salvation to the ends of the
>> earth.   (v. 6, NIV)

> When the time comes to save you, I will show you favor
>> and answer your cries for help.
> I will guard and protect you
>> and through you make a covenant with all peoples.
> I will let you settle once again

> in your land that is now laid waste.
> I will say to the prisoners, "Go free!"
>> and to those who are in darkness,
> "Come out to the light!" (vv. 8-9)

The new task which God has given the Servant is to bring God's justice to all the nations. God is Creator of the whole world. God is Ruler over all nations, not just Israel. God wants all nations (Gentile or Jew) to come into the covenant and find true peace and wholeness.

> One by one, people will say, "I am the LORD's."
> They will come to join the people of Israel.
> Each one will mark the name of the LORD on his arm
> and call himself one of God's people.
>> (Isaiah 44:5; see also Isaiah 45:22-23)

No longer are foreigners to be left out of the people of God (contrary to Deuteronomy 23:2-7; Ezra 9—10). Instead, they are to become part of the covenant people if they also observe the Sabbath (a time of freedom and justice) and faithfully keep the covenant. Isaiah 56:6-8 says:

> And the LORD says to those foreigners who become part of his people, who love him and serve him, who observe the Sabbath and faithfully keep his covenant: "I will bring you to Zion, my sacred hill, give you joy in my house of prayer, and accept the sacrifices you offer on my altar. My Temple will be called a house of prayer for the people of all nations." The Sovereign LORD, who has brought his people Israel home from exile, has promised that he will bring still other people to join them.

Establishing God's justice among all people will not be easy, Isaiah 52:13—53:12 reminds us. The Servant of Yahweh will suffer in trying to bring God's justice to the whole world. People will look down on and reject the Servant. The Servant must suffer and endure pain. But "after the suffering of his soul, he will see the light of life and be satisfied; by his knowledge my righteous [just] servant will justify [bring justice to] many, and he will bear [the burden of] their iniquities" (53:11, NIV).

However, the suffering of the Servant is not the last word. Because of what the Servant does, God will honor the Servant. God will let the Servant divide the spoils of the victor. There will be justice in that day of the Lord.

CHAPTER 6

Justice and the New Covenant Through Jesus

Jesus knew of this tradition of the day of the Lord. He saw it as the time when God would establish a reign of justice. Jesus knew of the task of the Servant, which was written in the book of Isaiah. In beginning his ministry, Jesus took on that task. At his baptism, the Spirit of God came to rest on Jesus. This is what Jesus announced in his sermon in Nazareth: that the Spirit of the Lord was upon *him*. God had chosen *him* to bring good news to the poor and set free the oppressed. Now was the time of God's grace, the day of the Lord, when God would save God's people (see Luke 4:15-21). Jesus took on the task of bringing God's justice.

It is often hard for us to see justice in the Gospels because we do not recognize the justice language there. Just as in the Old Testament, often the New Testament word for *justice* is translated as *righteousness* (or in the *Good News Bible*, "doing what God requires"). *Covenant* occurs only a few times.

But the New Testament is full of other language which

refers to doing justice and being in right relationship with God and with other people. This is the same kind of language we found in our Old Testament study of justice. The justice word we find most often in the Gospels is *faith* (in the noun form). "To have faith" or "to believe" is the same word in the verb form. In its Hebrew-Jewish life setting, it also means, "to be faithful to the covenant one has made."

To have faith in God is to be faithful to the covenant with God. Biblical faith is not just mentally saying yes to certain doctrines. Biblical faith involves not only the brain, but the hands and arms and feet. Biblical faith involves action that will keep God's people in right relationship with God.

In the Gospel of Mark, the message of Jesus begins, "The right time has come ... and the Kingdom of God is near! Turn away from your sins and believe [have faith in] the Good News!" (Mark 1:15). The purpose of writing the Gospel of John is stated this way: "that you may believe that Jesus is the Messiah, the Son of God, and that through your *faith* in him you may have life" (John 20:31). The ministry of Jesus was a call to faith, to faithfulness within God's covenant.

The Gospels summarize Jesus' ministry as teaching, preaching, and healing (Matthew 4:23; 9:35; Mark 1:39; Luke 6:17-19). Jesus not only told people about the kingdom of God. He showed it to them by healing the sick, casting out demons, and bringing outcasts like tax collectors and prostitutes into community.

In almost all the stories of Jesus healing someone, Jesus says, "Your faith has saved you," or "Your faith has made you well." For example, note the story of the woman whose menstrual flow had not stopped for 12 years. By

Jewish law and custom, that meant that she was continually "unclean." She was kept from active involvement in community life. Also, anyone else who touched her became unclean until he or she had gone through certain cleansing ceremonies. How alone and worthless she must have felt! The Gospel of Matthew tells the story.

> A woman who had suffered from severe bleeding for twelve years came up behind Jesus and touched the edge of his cloak. She said to herself, "If only I touch his cloak, I will get well [literally, be saved]." Jesus turned around and saw her, and said, "Courage, my daughter! Your faith has made you well [has saved you]." At that very moment the woman became well [was saved]. (Matthew 9:20-22)

This woman showed her faith in her action. She had faith that God would be faithful to the covenant to save the oppressed. So she acted. She touched Jesus' clothing (making him unclean, according to the law). She did this in the faith that, through Jesus, the salvation of God would come to her.

The story of the healing of the two blind men (Matthew 9:27-31) also emphasizes the faith of these men. They were healed "according to [their] faith." Like the woman in the previous story, they, too, had faith that God would be faithful to the covenant. They believed that God would hear the cries of those in need and act out of mercy. So they followed Jesus, crying, "Have mercy on us, Son of David."

The ministry of Jesus was a sign of God's faithfulness. Through word and action, Jesus announced that the kingdom of God was breaking into history now. The cries of the sick, the demon-possessed, sinners, Gentiles, women, and the poor were being heard. Through Jesus, God was bringing them into health, forgiveness, wholeness, and community. Through Jesus, they received healing, love, and mercy. They were brought back into relationship with God and others. Through Jesus, people saw God's intent for the Sabbath—-freeing the oppressed. The justice of God showed mercy to those who needed it most. It was the kind of justice that gave a party for the wayward son returning home (Luke 15:11-32). It celebrated finding the one lost coin (Luke 15:8-10).

That also is the message of the parable of the laborers in the vineyard, found in Matthew 20:1-16. A man hired workers early in the morning to work in his vineyard, and they agreed on the regular daily wage. But as the day went on, the man discovered he needed more workers. He kept on hiring them throughout the day, even until five o'clock, promising them a just wage. When the day ended, the foreman paid each worker the same wage. Then the ones who had worked all day complained.

But the owner answered, "I have not cheated you. After all, you agreed to do a day's work for one silver coin. I want to give this man who was hired last as much as I gave you. Don't I have the right to do as I wish with my own money? Or are you jealous because I am generous?"

The owner did justice to all the workers. Probably all were poor. If they had been landowners, they would have been working in their own vineyards. All needed the full day's wage in order to support their families. The justice of the owner was full of mercy and compassion for the poor and oppressed. That is the way it is in God's realm, said Jesus.

And that is the way it is among those who come into God's realm. Those who follow Jesus must be merciful just as God is merciful (Luke 6:36). Not only are they to love their friends, but they are to love and show mercy to enemies. Their mercy must reach out even to everyone, even those who do not seem to deserve it.

The disciples of Jesus are to follow Jesus in showing mercy, practicing justice, forgiving sinners, freeing the oppressed, and healing the sick. God will forgive them as they forgive others. But if they do not forgive others, neither will God forgive them (Matthew 6:12,14-15). God will judge them in the same way they judge others.

The other side of God's justice is judgment (in Greek, *krisis*; in Hebrew, *mishpat*). Judgment means life and salvation for the righteous. But judgment means anguish for others. The rich man who allowed the poor Lazarus to lie sick and hungry at his door was kept away from the side of Abraham after death (Luke 16:19-31). The rich will find it hard to enter God's realm (Luke 18:24-25). But those will be saved who, like the tax collector Zacchaeus, share their wealth with the poor and pay back those whom they have treated unjustly (Luke 19:1-10).

Jesus called people back to the true intent of *torah*. That was to help people live justly, to live in right relationship with God and others. Jesus did not do away with the law. Instead, he wanted to bring it to completeness. He said, "Unless your justice is greater than that of the teachers of the law and the Pharisees, you will never enter the kingdom of heaven" (Matthew 5:20).

The real intent of the law was to bring people back into right relationship with the brother and sister, the husband or the wife. God intended the law to help God's people tell the truth, confront nonviolently, love enemies, give alms (show mercy to the needy), forgive debtors.

The teaching of Jesus known as the Sermon on the Mount (Matthew 5—7) is like the law (*torah*). It gives direction to those who want to enter the reign of heaven (the realm where people are in covenant with God as Ruler). Those who are part of God's covenant are first poor in spirit, according to the Gospel of Matthew. Luke just says, "Blessed are you poor" (6:20). There is little difference in meaning here. In Jewish thought, the "poor" had come to mean also the "righteous." Zephaniah 2:3 says, "Seek the Lord, all you humble [poor] of the land, you who do what he commands." Psalm 69:32-33 also connects the poor with those who seek God. The poor in spirit are those who know they are in need of God's mercy.

Those who mourn are those who know about injustice, and they cry out in sorrow. A just God will comfort them.

Matthew 5:5 is better translated, "Blessed are the gentle." They do not try to bring about justice with violence, but wait on God to set things right. (See Psalm 37.)

God will satisfy those who "hunger and thirst for righteousness/justice." God will be merciful to those who show mercy to the poor and needy. God will be seen by those who are pure [clean] in heart, those for whom nothing is a barrier to a covenant relationship with God. Isaiah 1:10-20 says that God will not listen to the prayers and sacrifices of those who are doing wrong. But forgiveness [becoming clean] is possible for those who seek justice, encourage the oppressed, and defend the orphan and widow.

The peacemakers of Matthew 5:9 are those who are working to bring *shalom*. They are practicing justice and restoring right relationships, not sitting back to keep out of conflict. They are the ones who are like God.

But, warns Jesus, those who work for peace and justice may be persecuted. They will be insulted. People will tell lies about them. That is what happened to the prophets. And that is what happened to Jesus.

Jesus' actions for justice brought him into conflict with the religious leaders of his day. For them, righteousness/ justice had become following the letter of the law without the spirit of justice. They were not in right relationship with others, including the poor and the weak. Because Jesus did justice, he threatened their institutions and power structures. They could not understand that healing on the Sabbath was an act of justice in keeping with God's real purpose for the Sabbath. Jesus' mercy and justice showed up their lack of mercy and justice. So those who were in power wanted to get rid of Jesus.

Because they insisted, Jesus was killed. The Jewish religious leaders and the Roman political leaders worked together to have him executed by death on a cross.

Of all Jesus' acts of justice, his going to the cross was the most important. Through the cross, Jesus showed that he was willing to bring God's peace and justice and healing and forgiveness to the needy, even if it meant his death. Nothing had higher priority for him, not even saving his own life. No institution, whether religious or political, had the power to make him turn aside from God's way of acting justly.

In his death, Jesus was completely one with the poorest and most powerless of the world. On the cross, Jesus himself cried out for God's justice. Matthew 27:46 says, "At about three o'clock Jesus cried out with a loud shout, '*Eli, Eli, lema sabachthani?*' which means, 'My God, my God, why did you abandon me?' "

Jesus was quoting from Psalm 22. That psalm is a plea
for justice. It remembers how God was faithful and saved
the psalmist's ancestors. It vividly describes how the
psalmist is in danger of death. "O LORD, don't stay away
from me! Come quickly to my rescue!" the psalm pleads.
Then the psalmist will praise God in the assembly because
God "does not neglect the poor or ignore their suffering;
he does not turn away from them, but answers when they
call for help."

The Gospels understand Jesus' death as the beginning of
a new covenant between God and humanity. Like the
Sinai covenant, this new covenant began with crying. The
cries were the cries of those on the edge of Jewish society.
They were Gentiles, the sick, those possessed by demons,
women, the poor, sinners, tax collectors, and revolu-
tionaries. They all were crying for salvation from some kind
of oppression. Jesus heard and answered their cries.
Through his death, he amplified their cries; he made their
cries louder. His cry on the cross was a way of interceding
for them, of crying out on their behalf.

John Driver, in the book *Understanding the Atonement
for the Mission of the Church*, says that in Bible times,
people saw sacrifice as a way of interceding with God. In
Genesis 4:10, God tells Cain, "The voice of your brother
Abel's blood is crying to me from the ground." Isaiah 53:12
interprets the death of the Servant of Yahweh as "making
intercession for the transgressors." Hebrews 12:24 sees
Jesus' death in exactly that way. It says that Jesus is the one
who has arranged a new covenant. His sprinkled blood
"speaks more graciously than the blood of Abel." Jesus
interceded for others not only with words but with his
blood; that is, with his life. In his death, he cried out for

justice and forgiveness "for many."

The Gospels clearly understand Jesus' sacrificial death as the beginning of a new covenant. The covenant is ratified by sacrifice—and also by a meal. The Last Supper is the only setting in which the Gospels mention the word *covenant* (with the exception of Luke 1:72). As in ancient times, this new covenant between God and people was made valid with a meal. In the Gospel of Mark, Jesus told his disciples concerning the cup, "This is my blood of the covenant, which·is poured out for many" (Mark 14:24). Matthew adds, "for the forgiveness of sins" (26:28). Luke 22:20 phrases it, "This cup which is poured out for you is the new covenant in my blood."

In Luke, Jesus also tells his disciples,

> You are those who have stayed with me in my trials; as my Father has covenanted with me to give me a kingdom, so do I covenant with you that you may eat and drink at my table in my kingdom, and sit on thrones judging the twelve tribes of Israel. (22:28-30, author's translation)

The Gospel of John does not use the usual word for *covenant.* Instead it uses the word often translated *commandment.* But the sense of covenant is still there. In the long discussion by Jesus during the Last Supper, Jesus mentions the "new commandment" (13:34). This new commandment is connected with love that is willing to sacrifice even one's life. John 15:12-13 says, "My commandment is this: love one another, just as I love you. The greatest love a person can have for his friends is to give his life for them."

Jesus was faithful to the covenant by loving, even to

sacrificing his life. And God was also faithful to the covenant. God answered Jesus' cry for justice with the most powerful act of salvation yet. God responded with a "sign and wonder" beyond what the disciples expected. On the third day after Jesus died on the cross, God raised Jesus to life again.

The proper response of Jesus' disciples to the resurrection was faith: faith as action affirming the covenant. In the Gospel of John, the response of Peter and the "other disciple" to the empty tomb is faith (20:8). Faith is the response of Thomas to seeing the wounds of Jesus. The Gospel writer intends that such faith will be the response of all who read the Gospel (20:30-31).

That faith involves being faithful to the covenant in the same way that Jesus was faithful. The disciples are to love as Jesus loved, even laying down their lives for others. They are to take up their crosses and follow Jesus. They are to intercede for others. They are to bring justice and *shalom* to others. They are to cry out with their lives for those who cannot cry out loud enough on their own.

The way to true life is to have faith in Jesus—-to be faithful to God's covenant in the way that Jesus was faithful. John 3:16 phrases it, "For God loved the world so much that he gave his only Son, so that everyone who *has faith in* [lives in faithfulness to] him may not die but have eternal life."

In Jesus' death and resurrection, God made a new covenant with humanity. The new covenant is like the old covenant. It calls for justice for the poor and needy. It seeks health and wholeness for all. It offers God's mercy to all those who show mercy to others. It offers the blessings of being in right relationship with God and others.

But unlike the old covenant, the new covenant places no limits on justice. Not even death could stop Jesus from doing justice. Not even death could stop God from bringing salvation. Not even death can stop Jesus' followers crying to God for justice and acting to bring justice to others.

CHAPTER 7

Justification and the Household of God

The disciples had witnessed Jesus' death and resurrection. Now they wanted to understand what had happened. They needed to understand what Jesus' death and resurrection meant for them. The book of Acts and the Letters of the New Testament show the ways in which they understood this.

We cannot find just one way of understanding Jesus' death and resurrection in the New Testament. The early church used many different images to explain the meaning of the cross. The book of Hebrews speaks of Christ as both high priest and sacrifice, so effective that no more high priests are necessary. In Colossians 2:13-15, the crucified Christ is the hero of the winning side, leading the defeated powers of the universe in a victory parade. In Philippians 2:5-11, Jesus, who was a humble servant, even unto death, is now Lord of heaven and earth.

Some of the most important images in the book of Acts and in the Letters for understanding Jesus use a cluster of justice words. These are the ideas we have seen before: covenant, righteousness/justice, judge, judgment, love, mercy, grace, intercession (acting for someone else), and reconciliation (turning enemies into friends).

The apostle Paul passed on to the church in Corinth what had been handed down to him. He said that the communion meal was a way both of remembering and proclaiming the new covenant which Jesus had put into effect by his death (1 Corinthians 11:23-26). This was the central ritual in the early church. The "breaking of the bread" by followers of Jesus happened weekly in homes. In the Jerusalem church, it happened every day! (Acts 2:46).

By this new covenant they had become a nation, the people of God (1 Peter 2:9-10). They as the church were the bride of Christ. They had been brought into covenant relationship as in a marriage. Through Christ, they had been freed from slavery to the "elemental spirits of the universe." Now they were adopted as children of God (Galatians 4:1-7; Romans 8:12-17).

All of these images are covenant images. But the image that was used most often in the writings of the early church was the image of family, the image of the household of God. All believers were children of God. All had been adopted into God's family through the mercy of God toward them. They called each other "brother" and "sister." Elders called those in their care "little children" and "beloved" (see 1 John). They met in homes, and their house churches took on a sense of family (see Romans 16). As family to each other, they were to love each other, care for each other, and not lord it over each other.

Paul saw that the church was the family of God because the Spirit of Christ lived in them. No matter whether they were slave or free, Jew or Greek, male or female, all belonged to Christ, to one family. And because they were sons and daughters of God, God had sent the Spirit of Christ into their hearts, crying, *Abba* (the Aramaic word which means "Daddy"). (See Galatians 3:23—4:7.) The Spirit of Christ was the spirit of being family. It was the spirit of being in covenant relationship with God.

When the church received the Holy Spirit on Pentecost (see Acts 2), they received the power to do justice the way that Jesus had. The first believers (those who had come into covenant) had received God's mercy: forgiveness of sins and the gift of the Holy Spirit. They immediately began to create a community of worship, fellowship, teaching, and sharing of what they owned (Acts 2:41-47). They created a community where justice was practiced, where people were in right relationship with God and each other.

More than that, in the power of the Spirit, they continued the justice ministry of Jesus in preaching, teaching, and healing those outside the covenant community. Acts 3 reports that Peter and John healed a man lame from birth "in the name of Jesus Christ of Nazareth." Then Peter turned and spoke to the wondering crowd. The Jewish leaders arrested Peter and John for what they were teaching, and Peter, "filled with the Holy Spirit," preached boldly to the leaders. They went back to the community of believers, who then prayed,

> "And now, Lord, take notice of the threats they have made, and allow us, your servants, to speak your message with all boldness. Reach out your hand to heal, and grant that wonders and miracles may be performed through the name of your holy Servant Jesus." When they finished praying, the place where they were meeting was shaken. They were all filled with the Holy Spirit and began to proclaim God's message with boldness. The group of believers was one in

mind and heart. No one said that any of his belongings was
his own, but they all shared with one another everything
they had. (Acts 4:29-32)

The early church practiced justice both within the
church and outside of it. Those who had received the
mercy of God, now practiced mercy. They shared
everything they had with each other. They preached the
Word of God to all. They offered healing to the sick and
oppressed. This was justice in action. This was the work of
the Holy Spirit!

People sometimes argue that the economic sharing of
the Jerusalem church was a one-time happening—-and so,
not an example for us. But the New Testament church kept
on sharing their money and belongings in many ways. The
church took care of widows (see not only Acts 6, but also 1
Timothy 5:9-16). Paul collected money from the churches
in Macedonia and Achaia for the poor in the church in
Jerusalem (Romans 15:26; 2 Corinthians 8:1-5). They were
putting Jubilee into practice in new settings.

Women were involved in leading house churches
(Romans 16), in giving prophecies (1 Corinthians 11:5;
Acts 21:9), and in teaching (Acts 18:26). In spite of the
limitations of the culture, the church gave a broader role to
women than the Jewish synagogue had given.

Slaves were to be treated as brothers and sisters
(Philemon 16). There were to be no social class distinctions
in the church (James 2:1-13).

Both inside and outside the church, believers were to
share the mercy they had received from God with others.
They were to offer to others a right relationship with God
and with other people.

Paul believed that through Christ, they had been reconciled with God. They had been God's enemies because of their sin. But in mercy, God had reached out to them and offered them a relationship with God. God had made friends with them. Because of this, they had been given the task of bringing others into relationship with God. They were ambassadors for Christ, bringing people God's message: "Let God change you from enemies into friends." Paul said that Christ, who knew no sin, became a sin offering for our sake, so that by living "in Christ" (that is, in the Spirit of Christ) we might become the "righteousness" of God (2 Corinthians 5:13-21).

In other words, the church acts to bring about right relationship between God and people. In this way, they become the "righteousness" or "justice" of God. They offer the mercy of God to all. They are the living proof that God is just, that God wants to bring everyone into right relationship with God.

Bringing the justice and mercy of God to the world was no easier for the apostles than for Jesus. They were put into prison. They were beaten. People made fun of them. They were accused of things they did not do.

But they saw this suffering as a way of being together with Christ in his actions for people. Paul wrote in Philippians 3:8-11 that by sharing in Christ's sufferings, one would really know Christ and become like him:

> I reckon everything as complete loss for the sake of what is so much more valuable, the knowledge of Christ Jesus my Lord. For his sake I have thrown everything away; I consider it all as mere garbage, so that I may gain Christ and be [found in him]. I no longer have a righteousness of

my own [based on Law], but I now have the righteousness
that is given through faith in Christ, the righteousness that
comes from God and is based on faith. All I want is to know
Christ and to experience the power of his resurrection, to
share in his sufferings and become like him in his death, in
the hope that I myself will be raised from death to life.

Both the Letters and the book of Acts expected that
Christians would follow Christ in bringing God's justice to
others. They would show mercy as God showed mercy.
They would bring people to friendship with God. They
would suffer as Jesus had. They were to bring about justice,
like Jesus, by laying down their lives for others. That was
the way to glory, said Paul.

Since we are [God's] children, we will possess the blessings
he keeps for his people, and we will also possess with Christ
what God has kept for him; for if we share Christ's suffering, we will also share his glory.   (Romans 8:17)

One of the most difficult issues in the early church was
the reconciliation of Jewish Christians and Gentile Christians. It was difficult to take people of different religious
and ethnic backgrounds and include them in one new
community. They did not always agree on the right way to
do things. Sometimes Jewish Christians made Gentile
Christians feel left out, because they did not follow all of
the rules in the Jewish law.

Imagine that you are a member of a Christian house
church in Rome. Being in church has not been easy lately.
There has been so much conflict. The church may be the
family of God, but now the family is fighting.

There have always been some tensions between slaves

and free, between those who accept women's leadership and those who don't. But the major issue is between Jewish Christians and Gentile Christians.

The Jewish Christians are saying that we Gentile Christians must follow the Law of Moses as well as the new covenant. In practical terms, that means circumcision. Virtually none of the Gentile men in the church have been willing to undergo that. How important can a little piece of skin be to our covenant with God? What is really important is our faithfulness to the way of Jesus.

Then the Jewish Christians respond, "Jesus did not do away with the Law of Moses. Circumcision has been the sign of the covenant ever since the time of Abraham. Are we supposed to reject the faith of Abraham?"

You wish the church could get some clarity on this matter. When you get to Priscilla and Aquila's house for the gathering of the church, they tell you the news. A letter has come from Paul, the apostle. You hope he will have some guidance for the church on the issue of circumcision.

When the appointed time comes, Priscilla reads from Paul's letter. He writes, "Well, you say you share the faith of your father Abraham, whose faith was counted being right with the covenant. You need to remember that God gave Abraham a blessing before he was circumcised. It was his faithfulness to the covenant that counted, not the act of circumcision. Neither was Abraham saved by the law, because he lived before the law. So Abraham is the spiritual ancestor of everyone who shares the faith of Abraham—whether or not they are circumcised."

Everyone who has faith will be justified before God. Everyone who has faith will be in right relationship with

God. For there is no difference between Jew and Greek.
The same Lord is the Lord of everyone and blesses all who
call on God for help. For everyone who calls upon the name
of the Lord will be saved.

> (Adapted from the Letter to the Romans,
> chapters 4 and 10)

That is the social setting of the book of Romans. This
was a justice issue. How could people be justified (that is,
put into right relationship) if they could not think of themselves as one family in Christ? *To justify* comes from the
same root word as *justice*. *To justify* means to create relationships of covenant justice. It means to make people
"just" with regard to each other.

In the New Testament, *justification* does not mean a
legal action by which God calls us innocent when we really
are not. The justification Paul wanted for the Romans (and
for the Galatians) was the creation of a new community. In
this community, Jews and Gentiles would become one
family, one people, one body of Christ. Through Christ,
they all were sons and daughters of one God and so were
brothers and sisters to each other. They would be justified
with God and justified with each other. They would be acting with justice.

All people, Jews and Gentiles, said Paul, come into right
relationship with God and with each other by God's grace
and mercy. None are so righteous before God that they
could be in right relationship without Christ's intercession
and death on their behalf. God, through grace, calls people
into right relationship. Their response is to be faithful to
that relationship with God.

Following the ideas of Martin Luther, many people
have thought that the book of Romans says that *faith* and

works are opposites. But the difference between faith and works in Romans is not between thinking the right things and doing the right things. *Works* represents an attitude toward the Jewish law. In this attitude, righteousness meant merely following the rules. It meant living by the letter of the law. *Faith,* on the other hand, means *faithfulness.* Faith is faithful living in right relationship with God and others. It means living so that the covenant is not broken.

Paul says that people should not get rid of the law. Law is still a guide to living in covenant relationship. Law is *torah,* the wise guide which gives direction to living in justice. But the law takes second place to living in the Spirit. Such living puts covenant relationship ahead of just keeping the rules.

One way the Jewish Christians and Gentile Christians came into right relationship with each other was by not making Gentile Christian men be circumcised. Circumcision as a symbol of covenant living was less important than right relationships (justice) between Jews and Gentiles in the church.

Paul explains the relationship of the law and God's justice this way:

> But now God's justice has been shown separate from the law (although the law and the prophets give witness to it). Through the faithfulness of Jesus Christ, God's justice comes to all who are faithful. For there is no difference among people at all. All have sinned and are far away from the glory of God. All come into right relationship as a gift of God's grace, through being redeemed by Jesus Christ. God set him forth as a mercy seat through faithfulness unto death [in his blood]. God did this to show God's justice in

passing over past sins because of God's patience. This was to show God's justice in the present time. This was to show that God is just and is the one who creates right [just] relationship through the faithfulness of Jesus.

(Romans 3:21-26, author's translation)

God's justice under the old covenant had been visible in the law. Under the new covenant, the church saw God's justice through Jesus. Through Jesus' acts on their behalf, they were justified. They were brought into right relationship with God and with each other.

The apostle Paul saw that right relationships between Jewish Christians and Gentile Christians were necessary for living the way of Christ. That was one way the church could act out God's justice. They had found peace with God through Christ's love for them on the cross. Now they were to show that love to others, especially to those in the church, and to those with whom they disagreed. God had loved them, even while they were God's enemies. Now they also were to love enemies, even the ones close at hand in the church.

CHAPTER 8

Suffering and the Justice of God

Living justly was not easy for the New Testament churches. People in the church disagreed with each other and had to work at reconciliation. They could do this because of the power of the Spirit. That Spirit had called them all into covenant relationship with one parent, God. But suffering was not just the result of trying to live together with others in the church. The early followers of the way of Christ were persecuted by people outside the church. How could Christians talk about justice when they were oppressed? Where was God's justice?

Many Jews responded to the gospel message with favor on the day of Pentecost (Acts 2:41). But it was not long before the message of the apostles met with opposition. This opposition came in the form of arguments, legal restrictions, floggings, prison, and even death. At some point, Christians were told they could no longer be part of Jewish synagogues. Stephen was stoned. Shortly before the end of his life (A.D. 44), Herod Agrippa I, king in Jerusalem, executed James, the son of Zebedee, and put Peter into prison (Acts 12:1-5). We are told that his action "pleased the Jews" (v. 3). In A.D. 62, James, the brother of Jesus, was murdered by a mob.

The New Testament and other historical sources give many different reasons both Jews and Gentiles persecuted the followers of Jesus:

—They were teaching that Jesus had risen from the dead (Acts 4:2). . . . The healing miracles that the apostles were doing made the high priest and the Sadducees jealous (Acts 5:17). . . . Stephen was accused of "talking against our sacred Temple and the Law of Moses" (Acts 6:13). The high priest felt threatened by a new attitude toward the law.

—When many Jews in Palestine rebelled against Rome, beginning in A.D. 66, Christians refused to take up arms. Because of this, many other Jews called them traitors, and the Christians were forced to leave Jerusalem.

—In Jerusalem, a Jewish mob attacked Paul (Acts 21:27-36) because of a rumor that he had brought Gentiles beyond the barrier in the temple. There is no indication that the rumor was true. But it shows the threat that many Jews felt because Paul included Gentiles among God's people.

—In Philippi, the crowd turned against Paul and Silas because Paul had sent an evil spirit out of a slave girl. She had been earning money for her owners by telling fortunes, but now their living was ruined.

—In Ephesus, a group of silversmiths led a riot that threatened Paul's companions. These silversmiths had been making silver models of the temple of the goddess Artemis. They felt their livelihood was in danger from a religion that preached against worship of gods made by human hands (Acts 19:25-27).

The Roman administrators sometimes served law and

order by protecting Christians from mob violence (for example, Acts 21), but Rome could also persecute Christians. The Roman emperor Nero played on public dislike for Christians by accusing them of starting the great fire of Rome in A.D. 64. But all his decrees were nullified by the Senate after his death. Some Christians may also have suffered under the emperor Domitian.

The first concrete evidence of Christians suffering because they were Christians comes from the reign of the emperor Trajan (A.D. 98-117). To be a Christian was punishable by death. But Christians were usually not sought out. Their crime, as the Roman government saw it, was treason. Government officials offered to cancel the death sentence of those who agreed to burn incense on an altar to the emperor.

This new message of loving enemies, bringing justice and healing, and following the way of a crucified Jesus brought suffering to those who followed that way. To be a messenger of reconciliation often meant conflict. It often meant being misunderstood, for many of the reasons given for persecution were false. It could mean harassment, beating, imprisonment, or death.

The followers of the risen Jesus responded to this suffering in three ways. First, they kept on working for peace and justice. They kept on preaching about Jesus, through whom God made peace with humanity. They kept on healing the sick and casting out evil spirits. The gospel of peace was the right message, and they did not change it just because it was unpopular or brought persecution.

Second, the followers of Jesus' way suffered for the sake of justice, just as Jesus had. In fact, Paul saw that following Jesus required sharing in Jesus' sufferings. He wrote:

And now I am happy about my sufferings for you, for by
means of my physical sufferings I am helping to complete
what still remains of Christ's sufferings on behalf of his
body, the church.   (Colossians 1:24)

Many early Christians were willing to suffer for the
cause of God's justice because they saw that as the way to
God's blessings. If God's message through Christ was love
of enemies, how could they hate or kill enemies just to
avoid suffering? In Romans 12:9-21 Paul rephrases Jesus'
teaching on loving enemies, blessing persecutors, not taking revenge, and overcoming evil with good. (See also 1
Corinthians 4:8-13.)

Third, they could endure suffering because of their hope
that God would save them. This could mean being given
the words to say when they were put on trial (Matthew
10:18-20). It could mean miraculous rescue from prison
(Acts 12). Or it could mean faith that, just as God had acted
to raise Jesus from the dead, God would also raise them,
even though they died. They had faith that the way of loving enemies and bringing right relationships would win in
the end. Someday, in the time of God's final judgment, all
heaven and earth would know God's justice. The second
letter to the Thessalonians says,

We boast about the way you continue to endure and believe
through all the persecutions and sufferings you are expe-
riencing. All of this proves that God's judgment is just and
as a result you will become worthy of his Kingdom, for
which you are suffering. God will do what is right: he will
bring suffering on those who make you suffer, and he will
give relief to you who suffer and to us as well. He will do

this when the Lord Jesus appears from heaven with his mighty angels, with a flaming fire, to punish those who reject God and who do not obey the Good News about our Lord Jesus. They will suffer the punishment of eternal destruction, separated from the presence of the Lord and from his glorious might, when he comes on that Day to receive glory from all his people and honor from all who believe [have faith].   (2 Thessalonians 1:4-10)

The punishment of the wicked, in this passage, is not in contrast to merciful justice. Instead, it shows how God's justice will be established. It will happen in the same way that God has established justice within history—through mercy for those who call on God, through giving up the wicked to the consequences of their sin. The wicked, who have refused to come into God's presence in life, are not forced into God's presence in the final judgment. They remain separated from God and suffer the consequences of that separation. And they are prevented from doing more injustice.

Revelation 7:14-17 describes John's vision of the outcome for the martyrs, those who have died for their faith.

These are the people who have come safely through the terrible persecution. They have washed their robes and made them white with the blood of the Lamb [that is, they have shed their blood without being violent, just as the Lamb did]. That is why they stand before God's throne and serve him day and night in his temple. He who sits on the throne will protect them with his presence. Never again will they hunger or thirst; neither sun nor any scorching heat will burn them, because the Lamb, who is in the center of the throne, will be their shepherd, and he will guide them to springs of life-giving water. And God will wipe away every tear from their eyes.

The justice that these martyrs were denied on earth, they now find in heaven: enough to eat and drink, shelter, no more sadness.

The presence of God's Spirit which they knew in life, they now know more fully as they stand before God's throne.

The early Christians saw that the presence of God which they now experienced through the Spirit was just a preview of what they would experience in the day when God would finally set all things right. Paul wrote:

> I consider that what we suffer at this present time cannot be compared at all with the glory that is going to be revealed to us. All of creation waits with eager longing for God to reveal his [children]. . . . For we know that up to the present time all of creation groans with pain, like the pain of childbirth. But it is not just creation alone which groans; we who have the Spirit as the first of God's gifts also groan within ourselves as we wait for God to make us his [children] and set our whole being free.   (Romans 8:18-19, 22-23)

The early Christians believed that the power of God was stronger than the power of hatred, the power of governments, or the power of any opposition to the gospel. In spite of persecution, the church was not, and is not, discouraged. "We who have this spiritual treasure are like common clay pots, in order to show that the supreme power belongs to God, not to us" (2 Corinthians 4:7). Paul said that in spite of the constant danger of death for Jesus' sake, he had faith. "We know that God, who raised the

Lord Jesus to life, will also raise us up with Jesus and take us, together with you, into his presence" (2 Corinthians 4:14).

The early believers followed the way of Jesus. He worked to bring about justice without violence. He suffered torture and death rather than kill others. Jesus loved and forgave enemies. The believers had faith that someday it would be revealed to the whole world that victory belonged to the Lamb rather than to the beasts.

Their faith gave power to them as they lived out God's justice in the present and waited for God's justice in the future. Then they could sing with the saints the song of Moses and the song of the Lamb:

> Lord God Almighty,
>> how great and wonderful are your deeds!
> King of the nations,
>> how right [just] and true are your ways!
> Who will not stand in awe of you, Lord?
>> Who will refuse to declare your greatness?
>> You alone are holy.
> All the nations will come
>> and worship you,
>>> because your just actions are seen by all.
>>>>> (Revelation 15:3-4)

CHAPTER 9

The Church as a Community That Does Justice

How can the church practice biblical justice today? *The setting in which the church does justice is covenant community.* In our society, justice has come to mean many things. The government courts claim to do justice. Individuals or secular organizations may work for human rights. This work is good. But the better work of the church is to do justice in the context of a covenant community.

As the Bible understands it, justice means living rightly in a relationship which was created by covenant. The church, as the people of God, is to be that covenant community. That community is first a community of faith in God. Because God is full of grace and mercy toward us, God calls us into the family of God. God calls us even though we may have been far away from God and without good relationships at all. God has so much compassion and love for us. God wants us to be in relationship. God wants to show faithfulness to us, as God has promised to do. God wants us also to be faithful and to keep our promises.

The call to faith is not just a call to a faithful relationship
with God. It is also a call to faithful relationships with other
people. Because God has shown mercy toward us, we are to
show mercy toward others, even our enemies. Those
people in covenant with God are also in covenant with
each other. They are called to right relationships with each
other, to living justly. To be faithful to a God who defends
the widow, the orphan, and the oppressed, and who loves
enemies, means that we act with loving justice toward the
poor, the oppressed, and enemies.

God not only "walks with me and talks with me"; God
calls me to keep in step by acting as God acts. God forgives
me and expects me to forgive others. God loves me even
when I am acting like an enemy of God. Then God expects
me to love my enemies, whether close at hand or far away.
God heals me and therefore asks me to be a channel of
God's healing to others. God has a special concern for the
poor and so asks me to care for the poor. God works justice
for the oppressed and therefore asks me to work for justice.

God asks us to do this justice work not only because it is
part of the contract that we are obligated to keep. We do
justice because that is the way to stay connected with a just
God. We do justice out of our love for God and God's love
for us. Doing justice keeps us in right relationship with God
and others.

The people of God must practice justice first in rela-
tionships within the church itself. The early church tried to
reconcile Jewish Christians and Gentile Christians. In a
similar way, the church today works to reconcile groups
that are in conflict. It tries to bring them into right relationship with each other to achieve justice. It works at resolving
conflict because of race or class or gender, for in Christ

there is neither Jew nor Greek, slave nor free, male nor female (Galatians 3:27).

Justice within the church also involves just economic relationships—a special concern for those who are in need. It means living in community with people who are different, rather than excluding them because we feel uncomfortable with them. It involves various kinds of healing and reconciling ministries within the church. The church is not a place for perfect people—people who look as if they have life all together. In the church, we experience confession and forgiveness for our sins. We find healing for our physical and spiritual sickness. We find right relationship with our enemy close at hand. We find comfort for our sorrow, wisdom in exchange for our ignorance, and freedom from that which oppresses us.

Such a church constantly seeks to be in touch with the Spirit of Christ as it works at making relationships right within the church. This Spirit is a spirit of unity in spite of differences—of "many gifts but the same Spirit" (1 Corinthians 12:4). Because we in the church are all children of the same Abba in heaven, the church creates "family" relationships outside the biological family. Here people can feel that someone cares about them and that they have responsibility for the care of others. The inner life of this community in covenant with God is to be a sign in the world of God's justice.

The people of God also do justice on behalf of those outside the church. The church practices justice not only within its circle, but in the world. We find our model in Jesus, whose mission the Gospels define as preaching, teaching, and healing. All these are signs of God's reign. All these call others into the covenant community.

Preaching: The Greek word for preaching really means announcing. This is what a ruler's messengers do when they come into a city announcing the ruler's visit. The messenger announces (preaches) the message so the people can get ready for the visit.

Our task as the church is to announce that the reign of God has come and that God is calling all people into covenant relationship. God wants all people to live justly with each other.

To some, this announcement will come as the good news of freedom from oppression of some kind. It will be good news to the poor, to women, to minorities, to the troubled, to those looked down upon. For others, this announcement is a call to repentance, to turn away from sin and injustice, and come into right relationship with God and others. Both oppressed and oppressors are called to live in justice.

So the church "preaches" (announces) the invitation to covenant community to the oppressed and oppressors, to the powerless and the powerful, to the haves and the have-nots. It preaches in the slums and in the country clubs. It makes its announcement among the poor and the rich, whether in city or country.

The church calls all those outside the church, including those in secular government, to practice God's kind of justice. This is because the church claims that God's government has priority over all other governments. The church claims that only God's way of justice and enemy-loving mercy will bring lasting peace and community to the world. Ephesians 3:10 affirms that it is through the church that the governments and powers in the spiritual realms will learn of the wisdom of God.

Teaching: Teaching is also part of the justice mission of

the church. People need to know the Bible, to understand what it meant for those to whom it was written and what it means for us now. They need to know why justice is important to the biblical faith. They need to connect justice with the central message of the cross and resurrection of Jesus, instead of seeing justice as just one more commandment.

The best teaching happens through both reflection and action. People learn best when they are given a chance to reflect and discuss and plan—and then are given a chance to put those insights and plans into action. We learn through both thinking and doing. We cannot learn very much about the justice of God just by talking about it; we need to act with justice. Nor can we learn much just by doing, without a chance to reflect and evaluate. Jesus said, "If you love me, you will obey my commandments" (John 14:15). The Anabaptist writer Hans Denck in the sixteenth century expressed it this way: Whoever would know Christ must follow him in life, and whoever would follow him must already know him.

Healing: When Jesus healed people from sickness or sin or evil spirits, the crowds followed him. Healing was both an act of justice in itself and a way of calling people into God's community of covenant. In the same way, the church today must not only preach and teach, but heal in its mission to the world.

Healing is, first, a sign of the justice of God in the world. Jesus saw that casting out demons through his ministry was a sign that the reign of God was present. Likewise, the church in its mission announces the saving justice of God's reign to those who are poor, weak, and strangers. It offers healing to the sick and troubled. It offers forgiveness to sinners. It offers community to the lonely and alienated. It offers food to the hungry, shelter to the homeless, jobs to the unemployed. It offers peace and reconciliation to enemies. In this way the church becomes the righteousness (justice) of God (2 Corinthians 5:21). We offer God's healing and reconciliation because we who have received God's justice are now to be the channels of justice to others.

Second, such acts of justice, as well as words, are calls to join the covenant community. These actions say, Come into a community where people do justice to each other and to others and where you will experience justice. Evangelism (that is, announcing the good news of God's reign and inviting people to come into it) is not only a matter of preaching and teaching. Evangelism must also be connected with healing and doing justice to all.

Justice is clearly connected with evangelism in the Sermon on the Mount. There, in the Beatitudes, Jesus tells of the blessing for those who are peacemakers, who hunger and thirst for justice, who are persecuted for the sake of justice. Immediately following this are the words: "You are the salt of the earth. . . . You are the light of the world" (Matthew 5:13-16). Our saltiness, the brilliance of our light, is connected with doing justice and bringing peace. By doing these things, we bring glory to God and draw people closer to God.

The church is to call people to be reconciled to God and others—and then to become reconcilers themselves. The mercy they have received from God they can then share with others. We are not only to serve others, but to call them to become servants of Christ as well.

Intercession is an act of justice. Genesis 18 tells the story of Abraham as a person of justice. The Lord and the two men came to tell Abraham and Sarah that they would have a son. Before the Lord left, he told Abraham that he intended to destroy the cities of Sodom and Gomorrah because of their great sin. The Lord said to himself,

> I will not hide from Abraham what I am going to do. His descendants will become a great and mighty nation, and through him I will bless all the nations. I have chosen him in order that he may command his sons and his descendants to obey me and to do what is right and just. If they do, I will do everything for him that I have promised.
>
> (Genesis 18:17-19)

And Abraham did act with justice. He pleaded with the Lord to spare the city if only ten innocent people lived there. Abraham appealed to God's justice: "The judge of all the earth has to act justly" (v. 25). Abraham was just because he cried out to God on behalf of others. Through such acts of justice, blessing was to come to all the nations.

Abraham appealed to God's justice for one city. Jesus appealed to God's justice for the whole world. He offered up not only his cries, but his life so that all nations might receive blessing. That is the kind of life to which we are called as children of Abraham and followers of Jesus. Our words and our actions are to bring God's justice to the world.

We are people who have experienced God's salvation when we did not deserve it through Christ's cry on our behalf. Because of Jesus' intercession for us, we have received mercy, justice, healing, salvation, forgiveness, right relationships, and inclusion in the community of the new covenant. So now our calling is to cry to God on behalf of the oppressed. We are to follow Jesus in taking up both his ministry and his cross of suffering on behalf of others. We are to lay down our lives to save individuals, groups, enemies, even the world from destruction. We are to intercede, with our prayers and our actions, that through us all the peoples of the world might be blessed.

Like Jesus, we do this in confidence that God is just. We have faith that God will be faithful to the covenant, and in mercy will continue to save those who need God's justice.

The Spirit of God gives us the power to act for justice. According to Acts 1:8, the last words of the risen Jesus to the apostles were, "When the Holy Spirit comes upon you, you will be filled with power, and you will be witnesses for me in Jerusalem, in all of Judea and Samaria, and to the ends of the earth." The power of the Spirit enables us to act with justice and to witness to Jesus' life and death for justice.

The Spirit is our assurance that God is present and active in our lives. It is our assurance that we are in relationship with a God who loves us. The closer our relationship to God, the more we are connected with God's power. The more we sense God's power at work in us, the more we experience the release of that power through us for our own healing and the healing of the world.

The reverse is also true. As we work for justice, we come into closer relationship with God. We will be in better relationship with a God who does justice, when we, too, are making peace, loving and interceding for enemies, suffering for the sake of justice, announcing God's reign, and calling people to be part of it. We cannot hate our brother or sister and say we love God. Loving the neighbor and loving God go hand in hand.

The power of the Spirit, rather than guilt, keeps us working for justice in spite of difficulties. Guilt raises our awareness of injustice and helps us see where we need to repent, turn around, ask for forgiveness, and do something different. But guilt cannot sustain our action. Only the Spirit of a God who forgives us and calls us into relationship with those who are suffering can keep us working for justice. That Spirit in our prayer and in the lives of those who suffer gives us the energy to continue doing justice.

Living in the Spirit is not a matter of following certain rules. It means helping to establish right relationship— with God and with other people—by the Spirit God gives us. It means removing the inner and outer barriers to relationship with the God whom Jesus called *Abba*, "Daddy." It means being at peace with self and neighbor. It means being "in Christ," as the apostle Paul phrased it. This means living in the Spirit of Christ so closely that Christ is embodied in us. Then we can experience the closeness of relationship with God that goes beyond following rules and "being good." Then we have the power to do justice and suffer for justice, as Jesus did. Then we can have the hope of sharing the glory of God, as Jesus did.

That, says Paul, is the mystery hidden through the ages, but now revealed: Christ in you [in your sufferings] the hope of glory (Colossians 1:27). God's secret is Christ himself. Christ, in his life, death, and resurrection, is the key that opens all the hidden treasures of God's wisdom and knowledge.

The Spirit which we now have is, in fact, only one of the first installments on God's final salvation and justice. The apostles gave witness that God had raised Jesus from the dead. That was the first installment. Now we see the Spirit of the risen Jesus at work in the world. So we can hope that

God will keep the covenant with us and bring justice even more fully in the end.

Our hope in that final justice enables us to live in peace and justice now, in spite of how things look. It allows us to wait on God. It encourages us to keep on doing justice and making peace God's way even though evil may seem to be winning now.

We cannot save ourselves. We cannot save other people in our own strength alone. We are a means that God uses to work justice. But we also trust that God will use other people beside ourselves, and will use other works of the Spirit, to bring justice. We have faith that someday God's victory over evil will be apparent to all the world. That is what empowers us to do justice. Then we can affirm with the book of Isaiah:

> No one has ever heard or perceived with the ear,
> > nor has anyone seen a God except you,
> > who acts on behalf of those who wait on you.

> You introduce joy to those who do justice,
> > to those who remember your ways.
> > > (Isaiah 64:4-5a, author's translation)

For Further Reading

Books

Baird, J. Arthur. *The Justice of God in the Teaching of Jesus.* Philadelphia: Westminster Press, 1963.

Driver, John. *Understanding the Atonement for the Mission of the Church.* Scottdale, Pa.: Herald Press, 1986.

Patrick, Dale. *Old Testament Law.* Atlanta: John Knox Press, 1985.

Yoder, John H. *The Politics of Jesus.* Especially Chapter 11: "Justification by Grace Through Faith." Grand Rapids, Mich.: William B. Eerdmans Publishing Co., 1972.

Yoder, Perry B. *Shalom: The Bible's Word for Salvation, Justice, and Peace.* Newton, Kans.: Faith and Life Press, 1987.

Articles

Achtemeier, E. R. "Righteousness in the OT." *Interpreter's Dictionary of the Bible*. Vol. 4, Nashville: Abingdon, 1962, pp. 80-85.

Achtemeier, P. J. "Righteousness in the NT." *Interpreter's Dictionary of the Bible*. Vol. 4, Nashville: Abingdon, 1962, pp. 91-99.

Bianchi, Herman. "A Biblical Vision of Justice." Akron, Pa.: Mennonite Central Committee Office of Criminal Justice, 1984.

Lind, Millard C. "Law in the Old Testament." *Occasional Papers No. 3*. Elkhart, Ind.: Institute of Mennonite Studies, 1982, pp. 9-41.

_____ *Transformation of Justice: From Moses to Jesus*. Akron, Pa.: Mennonite Central Committee U.S. Office of Criminal Justice, 1986.

Toews, John E. "Some Theses Toward a Theology of Law in the New Testament." *Occasional Papers No. 3*. Elkhart, Ind.: Institute of Mennonite Studies, 1982, pp. 43-64.

Study Guides

"Justice and the Christian Witness." Study Report and Study Guide. Newton, Kans.: Faith and Life Press, and Scottdale, Pa.: Mennonite Publishing House, 1982.

Reardon, Ann Marie, and Chambers, Kate. *Called to Live Justly; Social Justice in Luke/Acts*. Kansas City, Mo.: Leaven Press, 1984.

The Author

Lois Barrett is mentor (teaching minister) for a cluster of house churches in Wichita, Kansas, known as Mennonite Church of the Servant. She also represents her congregation on Churches United for Peacemaking, a local organization of congregations working toward world peace.

Lois was born in Enid, Oklahoma, and raised in the home of a Christian Church (Disciples of Christ) minister. After completing high school in Sweetwater, Texas, she graduated from the University of Oklahoma in Norman. While at the university, she began to be involved in protests against the war in Vietnam. She then went to Wichita in 1969 as a Mennonite Voluntary Service worker. It was there she became acquainted with Mennonites and found a church that was clearly for peace in the world.

Since joining the Mennonite church in 1971, Lois has been a member of a Christian intentional community (1971-78) and has served as associate editor of *The Mennonite*, as news service director for the General Conference Mennonite Church (1971-77), and as editor of *The House Church* newsletter (1978-80; 1983-85).

She has worked on peace issues through Churches United for Peacemaking (1983 to present), as a member-at-large of the Mennonite Central Committee U.S. Peace Section (1980-83), and as a member of the central planning committee of New Call to Peacemaking, a cooperative effort of historic peace churches in the United States (1977-80).

She currently serves on the executive council of the Institute of Mennonite Studies. She is the author of *The Way God Fights* (Herald Press, 1987), *The Vision and the Reality* (Faith and Life Press, 1983), *Building the House Church* (Herald Press, 1986), *Questions About Peace* (Herald Press, 1987), and numerous magazine articles.

In 1980-83, Lois completed her seminary education at Associated Mennonite Biblical Seminaries, Elkhart, Indiana. She then returned to Wichita to minister with the Mennonite Church of the Servant. She and her husband, Thomas Mierau, have three children: Barbara, Susanna, and John.

PEACE AND JUSTICE SERIES

Edited by Elizabeth Showalter and J. Allen Brubaker

This series of books sets forth briefly and simply some important emphases of the Bible concerning war and peace and how to deal with conflict and injustice. The authors write from within the Anabaptist tradition. This includes viewing the Scriptures as a whole as the believing community discerns God's Word through the guidance of the Spirit.

Some of the titles reflect biblical, theological, or historical content; other titles in the series show how these principles and insights are lived out in daily life.

1. *The Way God Fights* by Lois Barrett
2. *How Christians Made Peace with War* by John Driver
3. *They Loved Their Enemies* by Marian Hostetler
4. *The Good News of Justice* by Hugo Zorrilla
5. *Freedom for the Captives* by José Gallardo
6. *When Kingdoms Clash* by Calvin E. Shenk
7. *Doing What Is Right* by Lois Barrett
8. *Making War and Making Peace* by Dennis Byler

The books in this series are published in North America by:

Herald Press
616 Walnut Avenue
Scottdale, PA 15683
USA

Herald Press
117 King Street, West
Kitchener, ON N2G 4M5
CANADA

Overseas persons wanting copies for distribution or permission to translate any of these titles into other languages should write to the Scottdale address listed above.